Wor

MW01233368

for

Jose Silva's Book

The Silva Mind Control Method

Created

By

Cosmic Publications

Note to Readers

This is an unofficial workbook summary & analysis of Jose Silva's book "*The Silva Mind Control Method*" designed to enrich your reading experience. Buy the original book on Amazon.

Cosmic Publications have not added or removed any information that would change or indicate a different view other than the views and opinions expressed by the author of the original work.

OUR FREE GIFT TO YOU

We understand that you didn't have to buy our summary, but because you did, we are very happy to give you something absolutely free.

Scan the QR Code to get free

Scan me

Contents

How to Use This Workbook

Our workbook is designed to accompany the original book by the original author. With that said, we strongly encourage you to purchase the original to get everything you can from our workbook.

Cosmic Publications has done its absolute best to bring you a comprehensive workbook with outlined chapters of the original for your convenience and study. Here, you will find chapter overviews, goal statements, key takeaways, check for understanding questions, reflection questions, action plans, plus a Self-Evaluation writing section for your own personal thoughts and growth.

CHAPTER OVERVIEW: The chapter overview is intended to be a "birds-eye view" of the chapter. Its purpose is to give you a starting point to focus on the overall theme of the chapter.

GOAL STATEMENT: The goals statement is your declaration as to what you will accomplish after you have completed reading the original chapter and finished our corresponding workbook chapter material. We recommend reading this statement out loud as well as internalizing it. Read this statement frequently so that you don't lose sight of the purpose of the chapter you are currently studying.

KEY TAKEAWAYS: Every chapter of the original is dissected and segmented into key takeaways for your convenience. They are outlined by number and come with details supporting each key takeaway. This portion is where you will refresh your knowledge on each chapter you have read from the original and should be reviewed as often as needed. We have made this portion an outline form and not a paragraphed summation. This allows your mind to organize the information better as you work through the material. We feel like an outline is much more conducive to learning and thus will allow you to retain much more of the information.

CHECK FOR UNDERSTANDING: In this section we provide simple True / False questions that will test your basic knowledge of the various topics discussed in the chapter. Use this as a baseline for your own comprehension as it will help with answering the following sections which are reflective in nature. Answers are provided in the reference section of the workbook.

REFLECTION QUESTIONS: Unlike the "Check for Understanding" section of the workbook, the reflection questions are not solely about the information in the chapter but are designed to help you reflect on the information on a personal level. The type of questions asked will bring out a thought-provoking inquiry, such as "How do you relate to the information?" "What do you think you have to do to achieve the result you are seeking." "Is the information covered encouraging, causing you to be nervous or excited?" We have designed this portion to be about you. So, we recommend you take the time to answer each one honestly, then after some time has passed, come back and answer them again to see where you are. Making photocopies of the questions may be helpful so that you can come back later and see your progress.

ACTION PLAN: It's not enough to just read and write about the lessons learned in the book but to act so that you can begin to improve your life.

In the action plan, we recommend attempting the activity within 24 hours of reading the chapter or as soon as an opportunity arises. We highly recommend spending at least one week trying to accomplish the action step. The action plan is your opportunity to establish a new norm for yourself, so don't take it lightly. Be brave and begin to implement the information provided. The action plan is where the rubber meets the road. You can do it.

SELF-EVALUATION: Accountability is essential when trying to make yourself better. In the self-evaluation section, write your experience with each chapter. How did it go? Did you have difficulties? Did you accomplish what you set out to do? Did you achieve the Goal Statement? Write your thoughts and feelings about what you were able to do with the lesson of the chapter. We hope that this section will be full of positive statements and helpful self-critique if need be.

FINALLY: It is our opinion that each chapter, along with its corresponding workbook material, be done on a per-week basis. If you can focus on one chapter per week and implement the action plan every day, you are more likely to maintain it beyond the workbook. You can change this to a few days if you prefer, but whatever you decide, stick to it. You got this!

THE SILVA MIND CONTROL METHOD IN A "NUTSHELL"

José Silva created the Silva Method, a self-help and mindfulness method. It purports to improve an individual's talents by encouraging relaxation, the growth of higher brain functions, and the development of psychic powers such as clairvoyance. The book highlights how your brain is an incredibly powerful instrument that functions at many levels or states both during the day and night. At the Beta stage, you are completely awake and aware of your surroundings. You are in a Theta state when you sleep. You are in an Alpha state or level of awareness when you are shortly before falling asleep or immediately after waking up. By practicing the techniques of controlling your mind and practicing mindfulness you can channel your inner derives and accomplish the heights of your dreams. Each state has distinct traits, and no one state is superior to another. However, using the level that naturally supports it makes it simpler to do certain tasks. One of your finest techniques for attaining your major goals is to use your imagination. The Silva Mind Control Method makes use of the power of the imagination through visualization methods. This mindfulness program will help you achieve your goals.

Chapter 1:
USING MORE OF YOUR MIND
IN SPECIAL WAYS

Chapter Overview

The chapter talks about how important it is to use The Silva Method to increase the peaceful state of mind. Since your brain works in a different way and from time to time it requires an extra degree of relaxation for it to fully utilize its brain power. The Silva Method gives you a certain degree of relaxation of the mind and body, and increases your creativity, and helps you in decision-making which is essential in your day-to-day life.

Read ahead to understand how you can employ this method in your life to be a better version of yourself.

Goal Statement

"I will start using my brain in special ways so that I can utilize its hidden potential."

Key Takeaways

1. **As you get increasingly acclimated to using this method, you will settle into a peaceful, self-assured state.**

Your brain is an incredibly strong tool that functions at various levels and has an immense capability that allows you to tailor it according to your needs. When you start using this method, you will realize how helpful it can be in your life. It takes you into a self-assured state of mind that gives you a certain peace of mind.

2. **The Silva Method gives you a certain degree of relaxation of the mind and body, and increases your creativity, and helps you in decision-making which is essential in your day-to-day life.**

   Making decisions is frequently an essential aspect of your day-to-day life. Even though you're not in a position of leadership, your capacity to make decisions may have an influence on your professional life as well as the overall success of your entire life in general. The Silva Method enables you to be not only optimistic in life but also helps you to be the best decision maker that ensures your success.

3. **Your need to try The Silva Method if you want to achieve the mediative state of mind.** The Silva Method takes you into a deep state of relaxation that is deeper than sleep yet with a distinct level of consciousness. It is, in reality, a transformed state of awareness that is employed in almost every contemplative practice and intense prayer. In this, you are given specific instructions regarding getting to your level or getting into Alpha and reaching that state of mind.

4. **In this method you try to use your brain in a special manner.**

   Your brains play a big role in what makes "you" you, and maintaining your brain in top shape may offer you a leg up on success, especially in your personal life and your professional career. If you want to enhance your brain capacity and learn how to use your brain in a way that takes you automatically steps ahead towards success, then you need to try this method out.

5. **You get to control your brain in a certain way that enhances your overall brain power.** Mind Control goes far further than this. It trains the learner to use this level of thinking to solve little and major issues. Learning how to take control of your mind and steer it away from undesired ideas is not simple. It requires a lot of effort and concentration. Your unpleasant thoughts may have an effect on you on some days. What is key is that you avoid thinking, "can I control your mind," because you absolutely can.

Check for Understanding

Let's check your understanding of the information discussed. Circle the correct answer. Check your answers in the Reference A section.

1. Meditation is a state of deep relaxation, deeper than sleep yet with a distinct level of consciousness.

   TRUE   **FALSE**

2. For meditation purposes special sort of type of medication is used.

   TRUE   **FALSE**

3. Mind Control trains the learner to use this level of thinking to solve issues, both little and major, heavy ones.

   TRUE   **FALSE**

4. With Mind Control training, you can enter Alpha at will while remaining completely attentive.

   TRUE   **FALSE**

5. With Mind Control training, helpful possibilities do not begin to increase at an exponential rate.

    TRUE   **FALSE**

Reflection Questions

1. Do you have the habit of using meditative techniques to get through your day? If yes, then give examples.

_____

_____

_____

_____

_____

_____

_____

2. Have you ever wondered whether you have utilized your brain in the manner that it needs to be utilized? If yes, then please elaborate.

_____

_____

_____

_____

_____

_____

_____

3. Have you ever used The Silva Method or any other meditative methods like this, and what have you felt after using it in your life?

_____

_____

_____

_____

_____

_____

_____

4. What are some other mind-controlling techniques that you may have employed in your life? List them.

_____

_____

_____

_____

_____

_____

_____

5. What advice would you give to your younger self? What modifications would you want to make?

_____

_____

_____

_____

_____

Action Plan

How difficult is it for you to find your balance these days? You may feel as if your attention may be drawn from one new item to the next and from one drama to the next. And it is this that keeps your brain working overtime! Try to jot down the things that you could eliminate from your life to lessen the stress.

_____

_____

_____

_____

_____

_____

_____

Self-Evaluation

Did this chapter help you in finding better control of yourself? Now that you know how to maintain better control of your life, do you feel more confident? Evaluate yourself whether you have been preparing better for things.

_____

_____

_____

Chapter 2:
MEET JOSE

Chapter Overview

The chapter highlights Jose's successful journey and discusses what he did to get where he is today. It also talks about how you can achieve success in your life if only you have the will and courage to do it, as Jose Silva, who never attended school. He embarked on a scientific expedition, as a result, helped pay for his degree. He found that reduced activity increased the brain's energy. This chapter also highlights how he taught his daughter to use ESP in a letter to Dr. J. B. Rhine and accentuates that it only takes courage to achieve any milestone.

Goal Statement

"I will take inspiration from Jose's life and will try to implement as much as I can in my life."

Key Takeaways

1. **Your mind is an incredibly potent tool. It has the power to alter your thoughts, feelings, behaviors, and even how you perceive the world.**

   Your thoughts are an extraordinarily powerful tool. It has the capacity to change the way you feel, act, think, and even how you perceive the outside world. The influence of this tool on your life and career is fundamental. You should utilize this tool.

2. **Changes to your thinking will also result in changes to your feelings, as well as the triggers that cause those sensations.**

   The triggers that cause those sensations to arise will go when you alter your thinking, which will also alter your feelings. You experience more mental calm as a result of both of these results. Make the decision to ponder your thoughts intentionally and actively. Become someone who has mental control; learn to master your mind.

3. **The Mind Control corporation is a profitable family business today, with most of its income going toward funding additional research and the group's rapid expansion.**

   For such a novel area of study, there was no university, foundation, or government funding available. The Mind Control organization is a successful family business today, with most of its revenues going toward funding additional research and the group's massive development. In all fifty states and thirty-four international countries, there are Mind Control lecturers or center locations.

4. **Your awareness of your body appears to be one way that mindfulness encourages people to develop healthier habits**.

   Your eating habits can benefit from mindfulness. According to studies, it may aid in lowering emotional and binge eating. You can better appreciate your meals and become more aware of your body's cues that it is time to eat by tuning in to your body. This body awareness appears to be one method by which mindfulness encourages individuals to develop healthier habits.

5. **The capacity for mind control enables positive self-change. It's true that you can improve both yourself and other people.**

Possessing mental control gives you the power to improve yourself. It's possible to improve oneself while also helping others. When you have complete control over your life, it is a wonderful sensation. Anyone who wishes to learn to regulate their thoughts should consider doing this. There are two opposite sides to everyone: pleasant and unpleasant. You can have complete control over your life if you learn to dominate your thoughts and recognize the area you are combating.

Check for Understanding

Let's check your understanding of the information discussed. Circle the correct answer. Check your answers in the Reference A section.

1. Jose Silva was born in Laredo, Texas, on August 14, 1914.

   TRUE   FALSE

2. Activities that led to the development of Mind Control required intense attention and vivid mental imagery.

   TRUE   FALSE

3. The perplexing situation prompted Jose to embark on a scientific study quest.

   TRUE   FALSE

4. Jose's father passed away when he was four.

   TRUE   FALSE

5. Jose created the training that is today required for anybody to utilize ESP in less than two years.

      TRUE   **FALSE**

Reflection Questions

1. Do you take any steps to get yourself ready for the tasks you undertake? If the answer is yes, outline your preparations.

_____

_____

_____

_____

_____

_____

_____

2. What suggestions would you give the self you were two years ago? What adaptations would you prefer to make?

_____

_____

_____

_____

_____

_____

_____

3. How should one strike a balance between attempting to change a situation and adjusting to it, in your opinion?

_____

_____

_____

_____

_____

_____

_____

4. How do you think Jose's story has inspired you?

_____

_____

_____

_____

_____

_____

_____

5. What changes do you think you could implement these changes in your life?

_____

_____

_____

_____

_____

Action Plan

Write down your weaknesses and your strengths side by side on a piece of paper and also write down the things that you can implement in your life from Jose's life. Think about how you can overcome your weaknesses and transform them into strengths.

WEAKNESSES   STRENGTHS

_____   _____

_____   _____

_____   _____

_____   _____

_____   _____

_____   _____

_____   _____

_____   _____

_____   _____

Self-Evaluation

Did this chapter contribute to your improved self-preparation? Evaluate the changes you see in yourself.

Chapter 3:
HOW TO MEDITATE

Chapter Overview

This chapter highlights the fact that self-meditation is the first step in Mind Control, where the mind sets free the body's healing powers. The more you meditate, the firmer the grasp you will have of a kind of inner peace so strong nothing in life will be able to shatter it. Meditation is an activity that is widely practiced throughout the world. Use your mind to train your brain to go quietly into Alpha and to attend exclusively to the job of creating a simple image more and more vividly.

Goal Statement

"I will begin to meditate from now on."

Key Takeaways

1. **Even if all you do is learn to meditate, you will still be able to solve difficulties.**
   Problems will still be solved even if you merely learn to meditate. In meditation, something lovely occurs, and the beauty you discover is soothing. A kind of inner calm so intense that nothing in life can disturb it. It will become more firmly in your grasp as you meditate and delve deeper within yourself.

2. **Being unable to bring your sentiments of remorse and rage with you while you meditate at the Alpha level is one of the benefits of meditation.**

   You will initially notice when you are meditating that your problems and emotions of guilt are vanished. The fact that you cannot bring your sentiments of shame and resentment with you while you meditate at the Alpha level is one of its many benefits. If these emotions arise, you will simply leave the meditative state. They will eventually spend more time away as time goes on, until eventually they are permanently gone.

3. **One method for obtaining mental peace and heightened awareness is meditation.**

   The practice of meditation serves as one of the ways to calm the mind and broaden consciousness. The Silva Method is one of the most well-known meditation techniques among many others. The advantages of the Silva Method of meditation are praised by many individuals.

4. **You have likely been in Alpha before without being particularly aware of it if you feel like nothing happened during this first exercise.**

   Use only one technique to exit your Alpha level, starting with the first time you do so. You will have more control over whether you come out impulsively as a result. Use the hundred-to-one method strategy for ten mornings. Then count just up to fifty, followed by twenty-five, then five.

5. **The limited control you have over your brain, despite the excellent work it occasionally performs for you, is unexpected.**

The brain is believed to move randomly from one thing to another like a drunken monkey. Considering the good job our brain occasionally does for us, it is astonishing how little control we actually have over it. However, other times it works behind our backs, cunningly producing a headache, then a rash, and finally an ulcer to top it all off. This brain is simply too strong to be allowed to go amok. You'll quickly realise that it can perform some amazing things for us once we learn how to train it with our minds.

Check for Understanding

Let's check your understanding of the information discussed. Circle the correct answer. Check your answers in the Reference A section.

1. Your ability to use mind control will increase as you develop your visualisation skills.

    TRUE   FALSE

2. "A happy stillness of mind," called by Rumi.

    TRUE   FALSE

3. Meditation is not necessary for obtaining mental peace.
    TRUE   FALSE

4. Meditation cause anxiety.

    TRUE   FALSE

5. The more you practise meditation, the more firmly you'll hold onto an inner calm that is so solid that nothing in life can shake it.

    TRUE   FALSE

Reflection Questions

1. How would practicing meditation improve your life?

_____

_____

_____

_____

_____

_____

_____

2. Does meditation support optimistic thought?

_____

_____

_____

_____

_____

_____

_____

3. How do you deal with challenges and interruptions when meditating?

_____

_____

_____

_____

_____

_____

_____

4. What happens if you start practicing meditation every day?

_____

_____

_____

_____

_____

_____

_____

5. Does meditation really improve your life?

_____

_____

_____

_____

_____

_____

_____

Action Plan

1. Make a space for meditation.
2. Integrate meditation into a routine activity.
3. Spend brief amounts of time in meditation experiencing no resistance.
4. Individuals should practice meditation alone. Group meditations may still be helpful despite this. Participating in group meditation may help you stay more committed to the practice and provide you access to a wealth of information.

Self-Evaluation

What have you learned about meditation in this chapter so far? How will you be able to employ meditative habits in your future? Do a self-evaluation and see how this can possibly help you in the future. Or, if you have already started, write down your experience and if it has made an impact on your life.

_____

_____

_____

_____

_____

_____

_____

_____

_____

_____

_____

_____

_____

_____

_____

_____

_____

_____

_____

_____

Chapter 4:
DYNAMIC MEDITATION

Chapter Overview

The chapter emphasizes that passive meditation can be done in numerous ways. Instead of focusing on a visual image, you can focus on a sound. The chapter also highlights different ways through which one individual can practice dynamic mediation in his/her life. All of the strategies, as well as various combinations of them, will get you to a state of peaceful meditative awareness.

Goal Statement

"I will try to implement the habit of dynamic meditation in my life."

Key Takeaways

1. **Other methods can be used to achieve the passive meditation you've just read about (and hopefully are going to experience.**

   There are numerous methods through which you can achieve calm mindfulness. Rather than focusing on a visual image, you can focus on a sound, such as OM, O N E, or A M E N, pronounced loudly or mentally, or the sensation of your breaths. You can concentrate on an energetic point in your body, on the rhythm of drums and dance, or on a booming Gregorian chant while gazing at a familiar portrayal of a religious ceremony. All of these strategies, as well as various combinations of them, will get you to a state of peaceful meditative awareness.

2. **Once you've entered the meditative state, it's not enough to just sit there and wait for something to happen.**

   Merely waiting for something to happen will not get anything done for sure. You need to take immediate action and the action might range from preparation to execution. If you wait for something to happen, it will never happen; instead, get out and do it. It is lovely and soothing, and it does help with your health, but they are little achievements in comparison to what is attainable. Go beyond passive meditation and train your mind for structured, energetic activity, which I think it was meant for, and you will be amazed at the results.

3. **There are some daily concerns that can be solved by this easy meditational practice.**

   With meditative techniques, you can easily handle setbacks in your day-to-day life. If you try to tune in to some type of intelligence that will aid in the wicked design while meditating, it will be as futile as trying to tune a radio to a channel that does not exist.

4. **Researchers believe that meditative approaches might assist not just negotiators and managers find creative solutions to difficulties, but also those who are sad or suffer from other mental diseases and can't see a way out of their problems.**

Check for Understanding

Let's check your understanding of the information discussed. Circle the correct answer. Check your answers in the Reference A section.

1. Dynamic mediation cannot be achieved from methods other than a visual images.

    TRUE   **FALSE**

2. Once you've used this strategy to attain your goal multiple times, the method will become connected in your mind with success, and the process will become more automatic.

    TRUE   **FALSE**

3. If you try to tune in to some type of intelligence that will aid in an evil plan while meditating, it will be as futile as trying to tune a radio to a channel that does not exist.

    TRUE   **FALSE**

4. Begin each challenge by briefly recalling your most recent successful experience. When a more successful experience comes along, discard the previous one and use the better one as your reference point.

    TRUE   **FALSE**

5. Time flows from left to right in the deeper depths of our thinking. In other words, we view the future to be on our left and the past to be on our right.

    TRUE   **FALSE**

Reflection Questions

1. Can you describe how the many stages of Dynamic Meditation affect one's body, heart, brain, and mind?

_____

_____

_____

_____

_____

_____

_____

2. What effect do you think meditation will have on your problems?

_____

_____

_____

_____

_____

_____

_____

3. Have you ever practiced dynamic mediation?

_____

_____

_____

_____

_____

_____

_____

4. Is it better to begin with sitting meditation or active meditation?

_____

_____

_____

_____

_____

_____

_____

5. How do you deal with distractions like pain and itching during meditation?

_____

_____

_____

_____

_____

_____

_____

Action Plan

This is the time to move beyond the passive meditation approach you just learned and learn to employ meditation proactively to address certain difficulties. You will now see why the simple practice of imagining an apple, or anything else, on a mental screen is so crucial. Now, before you proceed to your level, recall something pleasant, regardless of how insignificant, that occurred yesterday or today. Review it briefly in your head, then dive deep into your level and project the entire episode onto your mental screen. What were the sights, scents, sounds, and sensations like at the time?

Self-Evaluation

What are the most valuable things you've learned in this chapter that you can put into practice in your daily life? Evaluate yourself to determine where you stand.

_____

_____

_____

_____

_____

_____

_____

_____

_____

_____

Are you enjoying the book so far?

If so, please help us reach more readers by taking 30 seconds to write just a few words on Amazon by using the QR code below

Or, you can choose to leave one later...

Scan me

Chapter 5:
IMPROVING MEMORY

Chapter Overview

The chapter shows how essential it is for you to practice mind control techniques so that you can have an improved memory. There are times when people forget what they experienced or are experiencing that can leave a detrimental effect on their overall cognitive function. The chapter highlights different ways through which memory can be improved.

Goal Statement

"I will try to do my best to improve my memory and cognitive functions."

Key Takeaways

1. **You may utilize less of the phone book and greatly amaze your friends by using the memory tricks that Mind Control teaches.**
   The memory tricks covered in Mind Control may help us utilize phone books less while also wowing our friends. However, if I need a phone number, I search it up. Perhaps some Mind Control grads do utilize their abilities to recall phone numbers, but as I said in the last chapter, motivation is key to making things happen, and my

motivation to recall phone numbers is anything from ardent. My urge would increase if I had to go across town each time, I wanted a phone number.

2. **Because of the desire, belief, and expectancy trilogy, using mind control techniques for anything other than important issues is essentially unsound.**

   Because of the want, belief, and expectation trio, using mind control methods for anything other than vital issues is essentially wrong. How many of us, however, have memories that are as effective as we would like? If you have mastered the methods outlined in the previous two chapters, yours may already be improving in surprising ways. Your newly acquired capacity to recall details of the past while in Alpha has some carryover to Beta, so without making any additional efforts on your part, your mind may be operating differently for you. But there's still opportunity for development.

3. **The distinction between recall and memory is well-illustrated in the world of advertising.**

   We have a well-known example of the distinction between memory and recall from the world of advertising. Everybody watches TV advertisements. If we were asked to name five or ten that we saw in the last week, we could only name three or four at most since there are so many of them and they are so fleeting. Advertising effectively generates sales by getting us to "remember" a product at a level below consciousness.

4. **Because you were not there for it and it was not significant to you, you won't recall or remember this incident.**

A leaf is falling from a tree millions of kilometers away from where you are sitting.

Because you did not experience it and it was not significant to you, you will not remember or recall this occurrence. But our brains really save many more records than we are aware of. You are going through countless experiences while reading this book that you are not even aware of. You're so focused right now that you're not even aware of them

5. **Everything you think you could have forgotten has an event attached to it. If it's a name, the moment you heard or read it was the event.**

You may link whatever you think you might have forgotten with an occasion. If it's a name, the moment you heard or read it was the event. Once you know how to use your mental screen, all you have to do to remember an occurrence you think you've forgotten is picture the circumstances surrounding it.

Check for Understanding

Let's check your understanding of the information discussed. Circle the correct answer. Check your answers in the Reference A section.

1. The memory tricks covered in Mind Control may help us utilize phone books less while also wowing our friends.

   TRUE   FALSE

2. The distinction between memory and recall is not well-illustrated in the realm of advertising.

   TRUE   FALSE

3. Because of the want, belief, and expectation trio, it is often advisable to utilize mind control methods for situations other than serious ones.

   TRUE   FALSE

4. The mental screen is a mediocre method for simultaneously strengthening memory and imagery.

   TRUE   FALSE

5. The incident will be there if you use your mental screen to picture a previous event that occurred around the occurrence you think you've forgotten.

   TRUE   FALSE

Reflection Questions

1. Do you wonder whether stress and worry are having their toll on your capacity to recall and focus?

   _____

   _____

   _____

   _____

   _____

   _____

   _____

2. Are you feeling forgetful and concerned about your memory?

   _____

   _____

   _____

   _____

_____

_____

_____

3. Do you often confuse dates? If yes, then elaborate.

_____

_____

_____

_____

_____

_____

_____

4. How important do you think it is for you to improve your memory?

_____

_____

_____

_____

_____

_____

_____

5. Share some of your memory-improving strategies that you have already employed in your life.

_____

_____

_____

_____

_____

_____

_____

Action Plan

Now that you know that it is essential for you to practice mindfulness to improve your memory, make a checklist for actions you want to take to improve your memory. Concentrate your attention and avoid trying to cram things. If needed, try mnemonic devices. Also, try to visualize concepts.

_____

_____

_____

_____

_____

_____

_____

_____

_____

_____

_____

_____

_____

Self-Evaluation

Evaluate yourself and see how this habit of mindfulness has improved your memory. Did you have any difficulties or face any road blocks when trying to apply a more mindfulness approach to life? What did you learn, and how do you think this chapter has helped you?

_____

_____

_____

_____

_____

_____

_____

_____

_____

_____

_____

_____

_____

_____

_____

_____

_____

_____

_____

_____

Chapter 6:
SPEED LEARNING

Chapter Overview

The chapter focuses on the importance of learning and explains the two important techniques of learning which will help you to become a good learner. The first one is the speed learning technique which enables you to gain information by reading the data quickly. The second method is the three-finger technique which will increase your concentration and increase your learning level from alpha to theta. These techniques will aid you to control your mind and memorizing the information in a better manner.

Goal Statement

"I will practice speed learning by using three finger and speed learning techniques."

Key Takeaways

1. **You have to recall information by making mental screens which will help you to control your mind and memorize better**

   In order to remember things, you need to start making mental screens. Mental screens will help you to acquire information and data and help you to recall later. In this manner, you will increase your learning and this will help you to control your mind in a positive manner. It also aids you to better understand the information.

2. **You can increase your concentration by using the Three Finger learning technique and it will also help you to memorize information**

You can trigger a deeper level of understanding by using three finger technique for learning. It will increase your focus and help you to remember information easily. This technique will also help you to boost your memory by calming your mind and triggering high-level brain functions.

3. **You need to control your mind by reinforcing the information first by reading it and then by listening to it in your own voice**

If you want to memorize some piece of information you can practice your learning skills by managing your thoughts by first reading the material and then listening to in your own voice again and again. In this way, you will be able to memorize it quickly.

4. **By achieving the alpha and beta levels of learning you will enter into the theta level of learning with a deeper level of understanding**

You will become a good learner if you successfully pass the alpha and beta learning levels. It will help you to firmly grasp the information and you can easily recall it later. This technique is highly recommended for students and professionals who need to remember information and data.

5. **You should practice the speed learning technique in order to save time and become a fast learner**

You can save your time by skillfully practicing the speed learning method of learning and become a good learner. This technique of learning will help you to read a large amount of data and extract important information quickly.

Check for Understanding

Let's check your understanding of the information discussed. Circle the correct answer. Check your answers in the Reference A section.

1. You will miss some important information by using the speed learning technique.
    TRUE   FALSE

2. You can excel in learning by increasing your level of learning from alpha to theta.
    TRUE   FALSE

3. If you need to recall information, you have to control your mind in the best possible way.
    TRUE   FALSE

4. Theta level of learner is the lowest level in order to become a good learner.
    TRUE   FALSE

5. Three finger technique will help you to focus and relax your mind so that you can memorize things easily.
    TRUE   FALSE

Reflection Questions

1. Do you think you are a speed learner?

_____

_____

_____

_____

_____

_____

_____

2. Have you ever practiced the three-finger technique? If yes then explain your experience.

_____

_____

_____

_____

_____

_____

_____

3. Have you ever experienced the need for speed learning techniques?

_____

_____

_____

_____

_____

_____

_____

4. Do you know any other technique which can help others to memorize information quickly? If so, what are they?

_____

_____

_____

_____

_____

_____

_____

5. How are you planning to increase your learning skills in the future after reading this chapter?

_____

_____

_____

_____

_____

_____

_____

Action Plan

By considering all this information, you need to practice these speed learner techniques in your daily life. You have to improve your learning skills so that you can save your time. In this way, you can excel in your career and become a good learner. Decide when you will start implementing these techniques. Once you start, be mindful of any progress you are making.

Self-Evaluation

Do you think you can improve your learning skills by using speed learning and three learning techniques? What is your way forward to increase your concentration in learning? Do you think these techniques will help you to memorize things? What is your way forward if you need to recall something?

_____

_____

_____

_____

_____

_____

_____

_____

_____

_____

_____

Chapter 7:
CREATIVE SLEEP

Chapter Overview

Chapter seven talks about how most of us have experienced creative sleep at some point in our lives. You may recall a moment when you dreamt about a genuine issue you had in your life and the following morning understood how to cope with it. The following morning you had the answer ready to be implemented and address your issue. This is creative sleep, and the Silva technique may help you activate it on command. Thus, we will grow better day by day in deciphering the secret information that our subconscious provides us via dreaming.

Goal Statement

"I will make efforts to practice the
habits of creative sleep."

Key Takeaways

1. **The Dream Control technique Silva teaches consists of three phases, each requiring a degree of mental focus.**

   In addition to receiving knowledge about the pathology of our psyches, we solve difficulties in our daily lives when we interpret a dream that we pre-program. There are three stages to Dream Control, including a meditational level of mind. The first is to learn to recollect our dreams. Though many people claim they never dream, this is never the case. Even though we can't remember our dreams, everyone has them. Take away our dreams, and after a few days, mental and emotional issues kick in.

2. **The term "coincidence" is used in Mind Control without criticism, and we even give it a unique connotation. We refer to a sequence of events as a coincidence when they produce a beneficial outcome.**

   Though we give it a specific connotation, we have no issues with the term "coincidence" as it is used in Mind Control. We use the term "coincidence" to describe a string of uncanny circumstances that produce a beneficial outcome. We refer to it as an accident when they have a harmful outcome. Mind control teaches us how to create coincidences. The expression "just a coincidence" is not one the Silva Method uses.

3. **Freud believed that telepathy may flourish while people are asleep.**

   Freud said that telepathy may flourish in dreams, according to the research He had to explain the dream by adding that sleep fosters an environment that is conducive to hearing from higher intelligence. Here you may ponder if you should behave passively while waiting for the phone to ring.

4. **If you will be patient with Dream Control and practice, you will unearth one of your most precious mental resources.**

You would not really expect to become a lottery winner; it is in the nature of lotteries that very few wins. But it is in the essence of life that everyone can win considerably more than lotteries provide.

5. **During mindfulness before going to sleep, consider a problem that can be handled with knowledge or assistance.**

Review an issue that can be handled with knowledge or guidance during meditation before going to bed. Be sure that you actually care about solving it; foolish questions evoke ridiculous replies. Now program yourself with these words: "I want to experience a dream that will contain information to address the issue I have in mind. I will have such a dream, remember it, and comprehend it.

Check for Understanding

Let's check your understanding of the information discussed. Circle the correct answer. Check your answers in the Reference A section.

1. Dream Control technique demands focus of the individual.

   TRUE **FALSE**

2. Many people cannot even dream.

   TRUE **FALSE**

3. You do not need to write down what you recall of your dreams.

   TRUE **FALSE**

4. Creative sleep comes to most of us sporadically.

   TRUE **FALSE**

5. You can train yourself sufficiently by creating a dream upon falling asleep that will offer you the answers you want.

        TRUE   **FALSE**

Reflection Questions

1. Do you often have dreamless sleep? If yes, then how often do you experience it?

_____

_____

_____

_____

_____

_____

_____

2. How many hours of sleep do you think you should get each day?

_____

_____

_____

_____

_____

_____

3. Do you visualize your problems before you sleep?

_____

_____

_____
_____
_____
_____
_____

4. Do you feel refreshed after you have had your night's sleep?

_____
_____
_____
_____
_____
_____
_____

5. What are the most promising target factors for achieving a creative sleep state?

_____
_____
_____
_____
_____
_____

Action Plan

For this action plan you need to meditate before you sleep. You need to envision the difficulty you have. Then you must express mentally that you need some guidance or solution to your issue and that you will dream about this remedy. Start doing this habit daily and see the positive results in you.

Self-Evaluation

Evaluate yourself how these mindfulness and meditating techniques are improving your overall health. What happened the first night you attempted meditating before bed? What was the first thing you decide to solve using this method? Did you get any response? Overall, was it positive?

_____

_____

_____

_____

_____

_____

_____

_____

_____

_____

_____

_____

Chapter 8:
YOUR WORDS HAVE POWER

Chapter Overview

The chapter emphasizes the importance of using your words in a careful and thoughtful manner as they create an individual's own reality. The words you utter have weight as they have the ability to open up new possibilities or lock them off. The chapter furthermore talks about the immense power that the human brain encompasses as it is not a nuanced translator of our wishes rather it absorbs and retains information, and controls your body.

Goal Statement

"I will recognize the importance that the words entail and will learn to use words thoughtfully as they create reality."

Key Takeaways

1. **Your words do not represent reality in fact they create one.**

   The phrases you utter do not represent reality, rather they are something you conjure up. For Example, you are telling your brain you had a lemon when you read those words about the lemon, even if you do not intend it. Your brain has taken seriously and delivered the message to your salivary glands that the particular man is chewing on the lemons. As the words that come out of your mouth, therefore, create the reality you inhabit.

2. **The brain is not a delicate interpreter of your wishes rather it acquires and retains the information, and it operates our body.**

   The remainder of the nervous system functions as a network, relaying information from the brain to various regions of the body. This is accomplished by the spinal cord, which goes from the brain down to the back. It has threadlike nerves that connect to every organ and bodily part.

3. **Two factors contribute to the strength of your words one is your state of mind and the second is your amount of emotional connection with what you say.**

   There are two factors that overall contribute to the strength of your word first and foremost your mental state and your emotional connection with whatever you say about anything. When you say something with conviction that is illustrated in your stance. For example, I can't seem to obtain anything. When something is spoken with great emotion, it becomes true, lending credibility to the sensation

4. **If you wish to activate your body's recovery process, which could be slowed by negative thoughts then you need to repeat things.**

   There is indeed a lot of strong social psychology research that shows that we overestimate the importance of our body's recovery process and misunderstand the role of situational factors when determining why people act the way they do. The research shows that we can think of one thing at a time, and we need to concentrate on a thought before processing another thought.

5. **According to research, the power of your words is substantially boosted at meditative levels.**

   According to studies, mindfulness-based training increases executive attention. Practicing mindfulness and meditation promotes increased awareness and focused attention. Several studies show that the practice can help relieve stress, manage anxiety, reduce inflammation, and improve memory and concentration.

Check for Understanding

Let's check your understanding of the information discussed. Circle the correct answer. Check your answers in the Reference A section.

1. Your words do in fact reflect your reality.

   TRUE   FALSE

2. If you want to trigger your body's healing processes, which may be blocked by negative thoughts, then you do not repeat things.

   TRUE   FALSE

3. Even at levels of mind considerably deeper than those used in Mind Control, words are extraordinarily powerful.

   TRUE   FALSE

4. The mind has far more control over the body than is commonly acknowledged.

   . **TRUE   FALSE**

5. The brain is really a smart interpreter.

   TRUE   FALSE

Reflection Questions

1. How often do you meditate in a week?

   _____

   _____

   _____

   _____

   _____

   _____

   _____

2. Do you think you can concentrate well when you meditate?

   _____

   _____

   _____

   _____

   _____

   _____

   _____

3. Do you think you can develop emotional involvement with whatever you say? If yes, then elaborate on how you do it.

   _____

   _____

   _____

_____

_____

_____

_____

4. What factors do you think contribute to amplifying the relaxation process during the meditation process?

_____

_____

_____

_____

_____

_____

_____

5. Do you think you often use your words carefully?

_____

_____

_____

_____

_____

_____

_____

Action Plan

Make an action plan of utilizing your words more carefully as they hold immense power. Acknowledge that you have made quite a progress so say that Every day, in every way, that I am getting better, better, and better.

Self-Evaluation

Do you think by employing the repeating meditative method of saying things twice has made you take action in a certain way? How do you think this chapter has transformed your life and changed your perspective on overall meditative methods?

_____

_____

_____

_____

_____

_____

_____

_____

_____

_____

_____

_____

_____

Chapter 9:
THE POWER OF IMAGINATION

Chapter Overview

Chapter nine emphasizes the importance of exercising the power of your imagination in your life. The more you envision, the more powerful your brain becomes and the more power you have over your ideas. The chapter also highlights how the ability to imagine is essential for development, and some may think you are fantasizing today, but when you achieve your goals, the same people will begin to wish to be like you. Keep your ambitions high and your imagination going.

Goal Statement

"I will exercise the power of my imagination in order to be where I see myself."

Key Takeaways

1. **Your imaginative power helps you in accomplishing your goals no matter how unrealistic they might seem to someone.**

   All you need to achieve your goals is to have a vision of where you want to see yourself. If you have that particular vision and self-control then that can take you anywhere in the world to the heights of success. Imagination confiscates the objective instantly; it obtains what it desires.

2. **Self-control need an opponent to conquer before it can achieve its aim.**

It strives to be tough, but, like most toughies, crumbles when the going gets tough. There is a kinder, less difficult method to break harmful habits that are through creativity. The capacity to manage and adjust your responses in order to prevent unwanted behaviors, promote favorable ones, and achieve long-term goals is referred to as self-control. According to research, self-control is beneficial to one's health and well-being.

3. **If you really want something then you will devise a plan according to it with your reasons as to why you want to achieve this thing in particular.**

If you truly desire something, you will design a strategy to accomplish it. For example, If you want to reduce your weight, the very first step is to figure out the root of the issue, Is your issue one of overeating, under-exercising, or both? Singling out these factors will get you where you want to see yourself.

4. **As you strengthen your Mind Control in this and other areas, your whole mental state will improve, which will contribute significantly to greater bodily performance.**

You will notice that when you improve your Mind Control in this and other areas, your whole state of mind will improve, which will make a significant contribution to your body's smooth performance. You will start to feel more in control of your mind and body and your body will work at its optimum health.

5. **Modifying your beliefs about your physical activities, on the other hand, appears to be capable of changing your bodies.**

We also have the misconception that our bodies respond mechanically to physical training. We track our calorie intake, as well as the calories we burn on the treadmill. You will notice that simply switching your beliefs regarding your physical activity appears to be capable of modifying your body.

Check for Understanding

Let's check your understanding of the information discussed. Circle the correct answer. Check your answers in the Reference A section.

1. If you believe you want to quit a bad habit, you are most likely to quit it in the future.

    TRUE   FALSE

2. Thinking about your habit and making a solid decision to break it may free you from that habit altogether.

    TRUE   FALSE

3. In your future endeavours, if you set unreasonable expectations for you to accomplish then you can still achieve them anyway.

    TRUE   FALSE

4. You will receive what you want if you stimulate your imagination with belief, desire, and expectation, and teach it to picture your objectives so that you may see, feel, hear, taste, and touch them.

    TRUE   FALSE

5. Willpower is characterized as the capacity to accept short-term temptations in order to achieve long-term objectives.

TRUE   **FALSE**

Reflection Questions

1. Do you consider yourself imaginative? If yes, then please elaborate.

_____

_____

_____

_____

_____

_____

_____

2. If you have a vivid imagination then how frequently do you daydream in a day?

_____

_____

_____

_____

_____

_____

_____

3. What purpose do you think imagination serves in life for you?

_____

_____

4. Do you think adults tend to have stronger imaginations than children?

_____

_____

_____

_____

_____

_____

5. What sort of vision do you have of yourself and your future? And how do you plan to achieve it?

_____

_____

_____

_____

_____

_____

Action Plan

With all of this in consideration, make a visual screen in your mind and project a vision of where you are right now onto it. Allow it to vanish and, while mentally staring at the new you, envision how it would feel to get there. Below, write down what it would take for you to get there. You will have to work hard every day to keep yourself in check. As a result, plan ahead of time.

_____

_____

_____

_____

_____

_____

_____

_____

_____

_____

_____

_____

_____

_____

_____

_____

_____

_____

_____

Self-Evaluation

Do you think by employing the imagination in your daily routine has helped you in envisioning your future better? Has the above action plan made you more in control of your life? How do feel about the new vision you see of yourself? Do you feel more empowered and confident about your life and future in general?

_____

_____

_____

_____

_____

_____

_____

_____

_____

_____

_____

_____

_____

_____

_____

_____

_____

_____

_____

_____

Chapter 10:
USING YOUR MIND TO
IMPROVE YOUR HEALTH

Chapter Overview

Chapter ten explains how essential it is to control the mind for better health of your body. The body has a direct connection with your mind. These two have an unexplainable connection with each other so if you practice controlling your mind then you will be able to have good health as well. This chapter highlights the importance of practicing mindfulness and improving the overall health of your body.

Goal Statement

"I will use my mind in a way so that I can improve my overall health."

Key Takeaways

1. **Medical science is learning more and more about the connection between the body and the psyche.**

   There is a striking similarity in the outcomes of all the seemingly unconnected study that have found that the mind is a mysteriously powerful role. The research shows that the brain and body are linked via neural networks that are made up of transmitters, hormones, and chemicals. These pathways convey messages between the body and the brain, allowing us to govern our daily processes such as breathing, digestion, and pain sensations, as well as movement, thinking, and feeling.

2. **If only you could develop the habit of controlling your mind you will have a perfect body.**

   The mind-body link exists and has a significant influence on our overall well-being. Researchers are learning how to utilise it to treat both physical and mental illnesses. And we may learn to use the magic of the mind-body connection to improve our happiness and health in our own lives. What you put into your body has an effect on your mind and mental wellness. What you consume has the potential to prevent or reverse mental health issues so be mindful of whatever you eat. If you exercise the power of controlling your mind then you will be able to have the perfect body that you always envisioned you would have.

3. **When your self-healing abilities improve.**

   It is unavoidable that you are using your mind to improve your health. You already know enough to increase the body's repair powers with your thinking, allowing you to tackle ailments more effectively. When you practice mind control techniques you will notice that you'll need less medical treatment.

4. **You can practice self-healing with the help of six simple steps.**

   The first step through which you can practice self-healing is to start feeling and becoming a loving and forgiving person in Beta. This will very certainly need a complete mental cleansing. Next, you need to go to your level as this is a significant step. This alone is a significant step toward self-healing since, as the unpleasant work of the brain its guilts and angers is neutralized, and the system is liberated to perform what nature meant it to do: fix itself.

5. **Communicate your goal to cleanse your mind thoroughly, i.e., to use encouraging messages, to stay positive, and to become a caring, forgiving person.**

Communicate your intention to totally cleanse your mind and also employ optimistic words, to become a compassionate, forgiving person. Mentally go through the disease that is bothering you. Use the mental screen to visualize and experience the sickness. Fifth, swiftly dismiss this mental image of your ailment and imagine yourself entirely healed. Also, repeat to your inner self and start telling yourself, "Every day, in every aspect, I am growing better, better, and better."

Check for Understanding

Let's check your understanding of the information discussed. Circle the correct answer. Check your answers in the Reference A section.

1. The mind reveals itself to be a strangely weak force.

      TRUE   **FALSE**

2. With mind control, the perfection of the body can be achieved.

      TRUE   **FALSE**

3. In order to improve our body healing abilities, you need to apply your thoughts so that illness can be combated more efficiently.

   TRUE   **FALSE**

4. Many graduates describe that using Mind Control in times of emergency can increase bleeding and suffering.

   TRUE   **FALSE**

5. By controlling the mind, you can improve your overall bodily health.

   TRUE   **FALSE**

Reflection Questions

1. What additional little changes can you make to enhance your health?

_____

_____

_____

_____

_____

_____

_____

2. Do you personally feel that you take care of your physical health through proper diet and nutrition?

_____

_____

_____

_____

_____

_____

_____

3. Do you practice mindfulness techniques that help you connect your mind with your body?

_____

_____

_____

_____

_____

_____

_____

4. How do you think you can enhance your mind's connection with your body?

_____

_____

_____

_____

_____

_____

5. How do you think you can cleanse your mind and enhance positivity?

_____

_____

_____

_____

_____

_____

_____

Action Plan

Now that you know that controlling your mind is quite essential in the overall health of your mind and your body create a checklist for the strategies to accomplish your optimum health. Have a realistic approach to things and also consider the possible risks. Make a plan for getting to where you want to see yourself.

_____

_____

_____

_____

_____

_____

_____

_____

_____

_____

_____

_____

_____

Self-Evaluation

Was this chapter helpful to you? Were you able to use any new information you've learned so far in your life? Do you believe you are more prepared to achieve optimal health?

_____

_____

_____

_____

_____

_____

_____

_____

_____

_____

_____

_____

_____

_____

_____

_____

_____

_____

_____

_____

Chapter 11:
AN INTIMATE EXERCISE
FOR LOVERS

Chapter Overview

The chapter emphasizes the importance of having a certain degree of intimacy in a relationship. Intimacy is essential as it helps the partners open up about themselves and their feelings. The chapter highlights how discussing your feelings and emotions and laying down your defenses being vulnerable is an important faction in building a foundation for your relationship.

Goal Statement

"I will try to increase intimacy in my relationship by using the exercises mentioned in the chapter."

Key Takeaways

1. **Intimacy, I feel, is the finest basis for marriage and not the type that invades privacy, but the kind that comes from deep acceptance and empathy.**

2. In a relationship, intimacy is a sense of being near, emotionally attached, and supported. It entails being able to share a wide range of human thoughts, feelings, and experiences. It is being open and discussing your feelings and emotions, laying down your defenses, being vulnerable, and telling someone else how you feel and your aspirations and dreams. But this stage takes time, so patience from both sides is needed.

3. **You can experience a certain level of an emotional connection for your friends and with the people with whom you have had a connection with.**

   You will notice attachments will build through intensive and sustained meditation, Minds are intensely attentive to other minds and are softly affected by them in ways that are otherwise only known to those who have lived their entire lifetimes together. Most rapid intimacies are superficial and fake, leaving you feeling empty. However, you may feel as though you are connected to each other at times owing to a strong emotional connection.

4. **Attachments are created during profound and lengthy meditation.**

   Minds are acutely responsive and are softly touched by other minds in ways that are otherwise familiar only to individuals who have shared complete lives together. Most quick intimacies are shallow and fake, and they leave us feeling empty. However, at times we might feel as if we are connected to each other due to a powerful emotional connection.

5. **When two persons are physically near to one other, their energy fields converge.**

Everyone has an aura, which some people see as a slightly visible energy field encircling the body. This aura may be taught to us. Indeed, as a result of Mond Control training, many of Silva's graduates reported seeing their own and other auras. When two persons are physically near to one another, their energy fields overlap. Their form, intensity, color, and vibrations all fluctuate. This occurs in packed theatres, buses, and two-person mattresses. The more frequent the interaction, the more long-lasting the modification in auras.

6. **Prolonged physical distance will revert the process, which is obviously bad for the marriage's harmony.**

Physical proximity is vital in a marriage. Proximity helps individuals understand one another and discover their commonalities, which may lead to a friendship or a romantic partner. Proximity is more than simply geographic distance; it is also about functional distance, or how frequently we cross paths with people. According to experts, physical love or physical intimacy through embracing, kissing, and caressing is equally as important as communication in the establishment of romantic ties. This is why many couples suffer when they perceive a lack of physical closeness in their marriage.

Check for Understanding

Let's check your understanding of the information discussed. Circle the correct answer. Check your answers in the Reference A section.

1. Sex is not the only intimacy a couple needs.

    TRUE   **FALSE**

2. The finest basis for a marriage is the type that invades privacy, but the kind that comes from deep understanding and acceptance.

    TRUE   **FALSE**

3. It is quite rare for people to have a happy marriage.

    TRUE   **FALSE**

4. Connections are created during profound and lengthy meditation.

    TRUE   **FALSE**

5. When people are close to each other their negative energies are transferred.

    TRUE   **FALSE**

Reflection Questions

1. Is there something you've always wanted to attempt but are too afraid to?

    _____

    _____

    _____

    _____

    _____

    _____

    _____

2. Have you ever felt comfortable with your partner that you could share wherever you are feeling?

_____

_____

_____

_____

_____

_____

_____

3. What sort of intimacy have you accomplished with your partner?

_____

_____

_____

_____

_____

_____

_____

4. What are the factors that make or break a relationship according to you?

_____

_____

_____

_____

_____

_____

_____

5. How do you think you can achieve intimacy in your relationship?

_____

_____

_____

_____

_____

_____

Action Plan

To do an intimate exercise with your partner you will simply have to make time for your partner in your day. In this you will sit face to face and gaze into each other's eyes, envisioning the eyes to be a "window into the soul." This may sound corny but it does help build a certain level of Intimacy. As you become used to sitting and staring into each other's eyes, the activity becomes calming and contemplative. Put it to music and give yourself 4-5 minutes of timed attention. You will notice that your intimacy will increase as you gaze into each other's soul.

Self-Evaluation

What are the useful things you have learned in this chapter that you can practice in your practical life? Evaluate yourself and see whether you have been able to achieve intimacy in your relationship or not?

Are you enjoying the book so far?

If so, please help us reach more readers by taking 30 seconds to write just a few words on Amazon by using the QR code below

Or, you can choose to leave one later...

Scan me

Chapter 12:
YOU CAN PRACTICE ESP

Chapter Overview

The chapter emphasizes how with ESP one can improve psychic ability. With the increase in imagination, the psychic power also increases. The chapter highlights how important it is to increase imagination so that one can experience the true realm that lies behind psychic power.

Goal Statement

"I will practice ESP so that I can increase my psychic power."

Key Takeaways

1. **ESP has nothing to do with psychic ability.**
   There really is nothing heightened sensory about ESP. The term "perception" is appropriate for the type of trials done by J. B. Rhine at Duke University, in which percipients correctly predicted the turn of special cards, thereby ruling out chance. You project your consciousness to where the desired information is in the Mind Control, not just observe it. Perception is an overly passive term for what you do.

2. **As your imagination develops richer, so do your psychic powers.**

   You will notice that as your imagination develops stronger your psychic abilities will also increase. logic out of the way. As an exercise, the students are asked to mentally project themselves inside metal cubes or cylinders made of stainless steel, copper, brass, and lead, where they test for a fight, odor, color, temperature, and solidity, all at a fast enough rate to get logic out of the way.

3. **With Mind Control, you do more than just perceive.**

   Through Mind Control, you do more than just receive information rather you actively transmit your consciousness to the location of the desired information. As a result, in Mind Control, you refer to "Effective Sensory Projection." through which you can actively project your consciousness to the location of the desired information.

4. **You will be well on your way to practicing ESP once you have mastered all of the techniques in this book.**

   By the time you've perfected each of the strategies in this book, you'll be well on your way to practicing ESP. You will be able to access deep levels of mind while being completely awake, as well as picture objects and situations virtually with the totality of five-senses reality. These are the two entrances to the mental realm.

5. **You can practise ESP to improve your aim.**

   You may improve your aim by practicing ESP. The psychic can communicate with materials as well as people with greater precision. For example, Dick Mazza, a New York-based actor-singer, supplements his income by typing book manuscripts for authors and publishers. He misplaced a manuscript one day and urgently phoned a Mind Control graduate for assistance. He last experienced it when he entered a tiny church auditorium to practice a play, he claimed. A group of young morticians were departing; they had come to participate in graduation rituals.

Check for Understanding

Let's check your understanding of the information discussed. Circle the correct answer. Check your answers in the Reference A section.

1. The imaginative mind, has not been trained by a series of visualization exercises.

   TRUE   **FALSE**

2. Our psychic power decrease as our imagination increases.

   TRUE   **FALSE**

3. Mind Control trainees build laboratories of any size, form, and color they feel comfortable with in a particularly deep state of meditation.

   TRUE   **FALSE**

4. Your mental perception apparatus is divorced from visuals and symbols, as well as how near it is to language itself.

   TRUE   **FALSE**

5. You will not be able to access deep levels of mind with ESP.

   TRUE   **FALSE**

Reflection Questions

1. Have you ever practiced ESP in your life? If yes, then elaborate.

_____

_____

_____

_____

_____

_____

2. Did you know ESP existed before reading this chapter?

_____

_____

_____

_____

_____

_____

3. Have you ever tried any of your psychic powers?

_____

_____

_____

_____

_____

_____

4. Have you ever purchased a crystal or attempted dowsing and wondered if they actually work? If yes then elaborate.

_____

_____

_____

_____

_____

_____

_____

5. How do you think you can increase your psychic power and channel it in your daily life?

_____

_____

_____

_____

_____

_____

_____

Action Plan

To test your psychic energies, you need to allow your mind to choose the three regions of most attractiveness while scanning the body in this manner. Maintain a scanning pace of once per second and write down areas of interest as they appear. You'll feel like you're making it up, so write down anything that comes to your mind.

_____

_____

_____

_____

_____

_____

_____

_____

_____

_____

_____

_____

_____

_____

_____

_____

_____

_____

_____

_____

_____

Self-Evaluation

What are the useful things you have learned in this chapter that you can practice in your practical life? Evaluate yourself and see whether you have been able to attain the psychic energy in your life or not?

Chapter 13:
FORM YOUR OWN
PRACTICE GROUP

Chapter Overview

The concepts highlighted in this chapter are exercises can be done by yourself, but it will need consistent, extended, enjoyable application. You'll be prepared for the aforementioned case work in a month or two after you've mastered it. You will then need other people's assistance, but under very supervised circumstances. The chapter highlights that you need to work cases by yourself to develop awareness of daily life's subtle signals as opposed to only the more obvious ones of grave disease. Work on a distant subject instead of using a person who is there as a case.

Goal Statement

"I will make my own practice group."

Key Takeaways

1. **Make sure you are in a peaceful area where you won't be bothered or interrupted.**

   Take time to recognize what external and internal distractions are for you, and then take action to remove them. Internal distractions like hunger, fatigue, illness, and other distracting thoughts can interrupt your concentration as much as external distractions.

2. **You need to ensure that each group member has successfully completed and performed all of the activities in this book in their right sequence.**

Ascertain that each group member has finished and done all of the tasks in this book. You will make sure that every member of your group has successfully completed and carried out all of the tasks in this book in the proper order.

3. **Keep your group together, keep meetings and keep working cases together once everyone starts to succeed with cases on a regular basis.**

Hold your team together, keep meetings, and keep working cases together after everyone starts to succeed with cases on a regular basis. You'll become better and better at it, and one day soon you'll be able to handle instances on your own. As you do, you'll learn to pay attention to subtle signals from daily life rather than just the more obvious ones from acute sickness.

4. **Avoid breaking the news right away when you find an anomaly in a case you are working on.**

Do not inform them right away if you find anything unusual in the case you are working on. This is the doctor's duty. It is your responsibility to improve your psychic talents so that you may both legally and psychically assist them and others. Just mentally make the corrections you see fit. Correct mentally once you have mentally detected.

5. **There won't be any "ego excursions," so make that clear up front. Most likely, one member of the group will do phenomenally better than the others.**

Make a prior agreement that no "ego vacations" will be taken. At first Tins doesn't mean he is the "best" or in any way superior; he has just achieved first. Someone in the group will undoubtedly succeed more spectacularly than the others. Even while some people may not start using their psychic abilities until the fifth or sixth encounter, the slowest psychics often end up being the finest ones.

Check for Understanding

Let's check your understanding of the information discussed. Circle the correct answer. Check your answers in the Reference A section.

1. Ensure that you are in a quiet setting free from distractions.
   TRUE   FALSE
2. Once you've mastered it, you won't be ready for the aforementioned case work for another month or two.
   TRUE   FALSE
3. When you discover an abnormality in a case you are working on, you should announce it straight away.
   TRUE   FALSE
4. It is not necessary to check that each member of the group has completed all of the exercises in this book correctly and in the correct order.
   TRUE   FALSE

5. Do not use any of the existing people as an example. Working on someone remotely and doing this are two different things in legal terms.

      TRUE   **FALSE**

Reflection Questions

1. Do you think that you get distracted easily? What are some of those distractions?

_____

_____

_____

_____

_____

_____

_____

2. What measures do you intend to take in order to cut down distractions?

_____

_____

_____

_____

_____

_____

_____

3. Do you consider yourself a good leader? What strategies do you use to lead others?

_____

_____

_____

_____

_____

_____

_____

4. What strategies do you intend to use in order to maintain your authority over people?

_____

_____

_____

_____

_____

_____

_____

5. What is the easiest way to make people listen to you as a leader?

_____

_____

_____

_____

_____

_____

_____

Action Plan

1. Structure your approach in accordance with the circumstance you are in because you are aware that a matching plan is crucial for shifting. Consider your life after it has passed and ask yourself whether you have accomplished anything. If there is, you need to think back to the plan you utilized to deal with it. Maybe the plan failed as a consequence of the failure. Therefore, picture the whole situation with a plan that is specific to the end result.

2. You need to have a plan if you want to accomplish anything in your life. Consider a goal you have that you want to achieve soon, and make a plan to achieve it.

3. Keep achieving minor goals, and be proud of yourself when you reach significant milestones.

Write down your goal and plan

_____

_____

_____

_____

_____

_____

_____

_____

Self-Evaluation

Did you make a plan specific to your objectives? If so have you made strides forward in accomplishing your objective. Has this chapter helped you in your life? Did you pick up any new knowledge?

Chapter 14:
HOW TO HELP OTHERS WITH MIND CONTROL

Chapter Overview

The chapter focused on the use of mind control techniques to help others. It furthermore highlights that we can channel our inner psychic energies to help others in need. The feeling of healing others increases the sentiments of optimism and feeling of fulfilment as not everybody can help another person. You can in fact heal yourself by healing others as well.

Goal Statement

"I will exercise helping others using my mind control healing techniques in the best possible manner."

Key Takeaways

1. **You can achieve Physic healing by using your mental energy**

   You can achieve healing by controlling your mind. Your control of energy depends on how your mind functions. It depends on your habits of visualizing the situations. You can direct your energy in a positive or negative way by mental mapping. You will do something that can make your energy flow in that direction and it will result in the achievement of that goal.

2. **Your confidence is the key to your accomplishment.**

   In order to achieve healing, you need to have self-confidence. You should trust yourself that you have the ability to do the healing and only then you can be successful. For example, if you want to score well in an exam first you have to believe and trust your abilities to achieve a good score and you can do that only then you can score good results. Nothing can be achieved if you doubt yourself and have disbelief.

3. **You focus on your energies more effectively when your survival is at stake.**

   When you think that your survival is in danger then your energy can be utilized and transferred more efficiently. So, you are more focused when you know there is no other opportunity and your life is at stake. In order to heal yourself, you should be more focused and determined.

4. **You can boost your feeling of accomplishment by healing others. The more positive feedback from others you get the more positively you practice the healing therapy.**

   You can have a sense of accomplishment when you heal others and they say that they are better than before. It will give you a spark to trust your powers of healing and practice your healing more positively. You can get the real feeling of pleasure and happiness by helping others and comforting them.

5. **You can heal yourself by healing others.**

Helping others can benefit you directly or indirectly. Sometimes you feel that you cannot heal yourself in any manner. In such scenarios you can try to heal others by helping them treat their problems and in return you feel the positivity and happiness which makes you feel better. So, you can practice healing yourself indirectly by healing others.

Check for Understanding

Let's check your understanding of the information discussed. Circle the correct answer. Check your answers in the Reference A section.

1. You do not need confidence in yourself in order to heal.

   TRUE   **FALSE**

2. Your mind is in your absolute control.

   TRUE   **FALSE**

3. Healing powers can rise the feeling of accomplishment within you.

   TRUE   **FALSE**

4. You can heal a person by using your energy and transferring it to the other person which is called Physic healing.

   TRUE   **FALSE**

5. Controlling your thoughts can help you heal.

   TRUE   **FALSE**

Reflection Questions

1. How do you think you can achieve healing in your life? What steps can you take to accomplish this?

_____

_____

_____

_____

_____

_____

2. Have you ever practiced any healing technique? If yes than please elaborate.

_____

_____

_____

_____

_____

_____

3. Do you think healing others is as important as to heal yourself? Explain your answer.

_____

_____

_____

_____

_____

_____

_____

4. What are the key benefits of using mind controlling methods to help
    others?

_____

_____

_____

_____

_____

_____

_____

5. What is your healing process when you feel discomfort?

_____

_____

_____

_____

_____

_____

_____

Action Plan

By keeping all that in mind, write down your healing process. Note down the ways to help others and make them feel better. Start appreciating yourself and have confidence. You are doing a very good job and you will do a lot better in the future.

_____

_____

_____

_____

_____

_____

_____

_____

_____

_____

_____

_____

_____

_____

_____

_____

_____

_____

_____

_____

_____

Self-Evaluation

Do you think you can contribute to your community by helping others? How can you improve your mental mapping in order to achieve better focus? Can you make a plan for yourself by writing down all the necessary changes you need to make in your daily routine in order to achieve healing?

_____

_____

_____

_____

_____

_____

_____

_____

_____

_____

_____

_____

_____

_____

_____

_____

_____

_____

_____

_____

Chapter 15:
SOME SPECULATIONS

Chapter Overview

The chapter illustrates that the predominant goal of the Mind Control course is to teach you how to address the difficulties that plague every human existence by using more of your mind in unique ways. There are many instances in the chapter that teach you to be more mindful of what you are doing in this way it enables you to practice mindfulness in your day-to-day routine.

Goal Statement

"I will make efforts to practice the habit of practicing mindfulness."

Key Takeaways

1. **Sir David Attenborough writes in his autobiography, The Great British Batsman's Guide to the World's Forests, "I have maintained my work on a very practical level, probably because I was born quite poor and life confronted me with practical issues from the beginning."**

The research in the chapter is the result of more than 30 years of study and testing. One of the most striking aspects is the lack of any genuine contradiction between what the investigation has discovered to be truly practical to religious beliefs. The Mind Control course, is especially designed to urge you to use more of your mind.

2. **There has been a troubling connection between science and religion for many centuries. The fact that the results did not contradict with any other religion or, in fact, with any widely accepted worldview is all the more astounding.**

   Science and religion have had a tense history together for millennia. Atheists, Protestants of all denominations, Catholics, Jews, Moslems, Buddhists, and Hindus, as well as scientists and academics from a variety of fields, are among our passionate alumni.

3. **Energy underlies everything. Frequency, or what energy is doing and how quickly, is what distinguishes one object from another. As we learn from the equation $E = MC^2$, matter is also energy; it is energy doing something else, being in another condition.**

   There is no opposite for energy, which is intriguing in a world where there are many opposites: up and down, black and white, quick and slow. This is so because everything, including you, and everything we believe, is made of energy. Energy is used and created when we think, or, to put it another way, energy is converted when we think.

4. **The universe appears to work with astonishing efficiency and creates no waste. You find it difficult to understand that putting one foot in front of the other is God's or Higher Intelligence's business; rather, it is yours.**

There doesn't seem to be a shred of waste in the cosmos, which appears to operate with astounding efficiency. You find it hard to accept that God, or, for that matter, Higher Intelligence, is concerned with making sure you don't trip when you put one foot in front of the other. You are genetically predisposed to develop your ability to walk; this was God's doing. You can take care of the usual procedures now that you've learnt them. But because certain life decisions are not predictable, you could require knowledge that is not perceptible to my five senses. You look to Higher Intelligence for this. You sometimes need broad, life-changing counsel. This is why you pray to God.

5. **One more of the hypothesis is that considering your lengthy evolutionary history, we humans have only just reached the end of a stage.**

   We humans have only just finished an evolutionary stage when seen in the context of our extensive evolutionary history. This was how your brain evolved. You have used up all of your brain cells, therefore this is finished and done. The growth of your intellect is already taking place as the next phase.

Check for Understanding

Let's check your understanding of the information discussed. Circle the correct answer. Check your answers in the Reference A section.

1. What you just read is the result of more than 30 years of study and testing.

    TRUE   **FALSE**

2. There is an opposite to energy that you use every day.

    TRUE   **FALSE**

3. Certain life decisions are always predictable.

    TRUE   **FALSE**

4. There appears to be waste in the universe, which appears to work with remarkable efficiency.

    TRUE   **FALSE**

5. We've used up all of our brain cells, so this is done and dusted. The next stage of our intellectual development is already underway.

    TRUE   **FALSE**

Reflection Questions

1. Do you take any precautions to prepare for the duties you undertake? If you answered yes, what are those precautions and are they effective? If not, do you think you would benefit from being more prepared?

    _____

    _____

    _____

_____

_____

_____

_____

2. What advice would you give to the self you were two years ago? What changes would you want to see?

_____

_____

_____

_____

_____

_____

_____

3. In your perspective, how should one find a balance between striving to alter a situation and adapting to it?

_____

_____

_____

_____

_____

_____

_____

4. In what ways do you believe Jose's narrative has influenced you?

_____

_____

_____

_____

_____

_____

_____

5. How do you believe you will apply these changes in your life?

_____

_____

_____

_____

_____

_____

Action Plan

Below, list your weaknesses and strengths side by side, as well as the things you can incorporate in your life from Jose's life. Consider how you may overcome your flaws and turn them into strengths. Then make a plan on how you can prepare yourself to accomplish these new changes in your life.

_____

_____

_____

Self-Evaluation

Did this chapter help you improve your self-preparation? Examine the changes you notice in yourself. Evaluate yourself how these mindfulness and meditating techniques are improving your overall health.

_____

_____

_____

_____

_____

_____

_____

_____

_____

_____

_____

_____

_____

_____

_____

_____

_____

_____

_____

_____

_____

_____

Chapter 16:
A CHECKLIST

Chapter Overview

The chapter highlights all the major things listed in Chapter 3 through 14 for readers to go through them. With a fast examination of those you may have overlooked, you may simply rediscover the knack and the positive outcomes.

Reflection Questions

1. Looking at chapter 3 through 5, what was the one thing you have learned that has stayed with you, and how has it impacted your life, or perhaps changed your perspective?

_____

_____

_____

_____

_____

_____

_____

2. What has been that special nugget from chapter 6 through 8 that has provided the most positive change?

_____

_____

_____

_____

_____

_____

_____

3. Looking back at chapters 9, 10, and 11, which one was the most intriguing? And, in what way did that chapter help you now that some time has passed?

_____

_____

_____

_____

_____

_____

_____

4. Chapters 12 – *You Can Practice ESP*, Chapter 13 – *Form Your Own Practice Group*, and Chapter 14 – *Helping Others With Mind Control*. Which chapter did you feel nervous about trying? What is it about that chapter's lesson that makes you nervous? Do you think there is a Mind Control technique that can help you overcome your hesitation?

_____

_____

_____

_____

_____

_____

_____

Action Plan

If you have not started any of the techniques discussed in the book start today. If you have, take it to the next level by setting more time aside to practice. If you do 20 minutes, go 25 minutes. If you practice 3 times a week, see if you can do 4 times a week. Every minute you spend practicing will get you closer to your goals.

Self-Evaluation

Write down all the obstacles you have faced while trying to implement the Silva Mind Control Method. Also, write down any achievements you have made so far. And finally, write down the things that you have yet to achieve and how you plan on achieving them.

_____

_____

_____

_____

_____

_____

_____

_____

_____

_____

_____

_____

_____

_____

_____

_____

_____

_____

_____

_____

Chapter 17:
A PSYCHIATRIST WORKS WITH MIND CONTROL

Chapter Overview

Chapter 17 emphasizes that the psychiatrist utilizes the power of controlling the individual's brain in a certain way. The chapter also includes different experiments conducted by the psychiatrist as they conclude what method works better for their patients.

Goal Statement

"I will try to control my mind as a psychiatrist does."

Key Takeaways

1. **Everyone seemed to have a mind-expanding experience, a realization that they could utilize their minds in new ways.**

   Those who continued to exercise Mind Control after the training were able to significantly transform their life, and even those who did not use it were able to apply it in times of crisis, whether dealing with stress or making vital decisions. It appeared to be a mind-expanding event for everyone, a realization that they could use their minds in new ways. The group's excitement grew near the end of the course, and most people felt a surge of emotional energy.

2. **Mind Control's safety has been put to the test by a member of the medical profession.**

   Dr. Clancy D. McKenzie is a well-known Philadelphia psychiatrist and psychoanalyst, the head of the Philadelphia Psychiatric Consultation Service, a member of The Philadelphia Psychiatric Centre's faculty, and an active private practitioner. In 1970, he participated in the Mind Control course as part of his study in these subjects.

3. **According to Freud, the most promising future path for psychotherapy is mobilization of the patient's energy.**

   Freud stated that the most promising future direction for psychotherapy is the mobilization of the patient's energy. Dr. McKenzie saw students in the Mind Control class employing energy they were unaware they had.

4. **Through his research, Dr. McKenzie found that there was a stronger sense of calm and less anxiousness. Patients gained confidence as they learned to rely on their own abilities to understand, cope with, and solve difficulties.**

5. **Researchers believe that meditative approaches might assist not just negotiators and managers find creative solutions to difficulties, but also those who are sad or suffer from other mental diseases and can't see a way out of their problems.**

Check for Understanding

Let's check your understanding of the information discussed. Circle the correct answer. Check your answers in the Reference A section.

1. According to Jose and others close to him in charge of the Mind Control organization, the training's advantages have yet to be shown the simplest method to compensate for any "unwanted side effects," to use a medical term.

   TRUE   **FALSE**

2. Another item that piqued Dr. Clancy's interest in Mind Control was a remark made by Sigmund Freud at the end of his career, and something that occurred in a Mind Control class.

   TRUE   **FALSE**

3. According to Freud, the most promising future path for psychotherapy is not the mobilization of the patient's energy.

   TRUE   **FALSE**

4. He assessed 58 of these individuals before and after the course to determine what changes it could bring.

   TRUE   **FALSE**

5. Psychoses are serious mental illnesses.

   TRUE   **FALSE**

Reflection Questions

1. What have you learned from the experiments conducted in this chapter so far?

_____

_____

_____

_____

_____

_____

_____

2. Have you ever been to a psychiatrist for your problems? If yes, then elaborate.

_____

_____

_____

_____

_____

_____

_____

3. How do you personally think counseling is necessary for a sound mind?

_____

_____

_____

_____

_____

_____

_____

4. Do you think a person should reach out to the experts such as psychiatrists for personal problems? Why do you think people shy away from seeing professional help?

_____

_____

_____

_____

_____

_____

_____

5. How important do you think it is to seek proper medical attention at the time of need?

_____

_____

_____

_____

_____

_____

_____

Action Plan

Create a plan of the various ways you can practice mind control in your life and practically implement them. See how far have you come in your journey towards mind control. If you have already begun, then come up with a new way you can use mind control.

Self-Evaluation

What are the most important things you've learned in this chapter that you can apply in your daily life? Describe some of your experiences so far with mind control. How do you see yourself progressing, and are you happy where you are at the moment?

_____

_____

_____

_____

_____

_____

_____

_____

_____

_____

_____

_____

_____

_____

Chapter 18:
YOUR SELF-ESTEEM WILL SOAR

Chapter Overview

The chapter focuses on the importance of self-worth and how it will help to achieve your goals. It also explains how you can experience the freedom of ideas and exposure by setting yourself free from narrow ideas and limits. It also discusses how you can boost your self-esteem by self-evaluation and criticism instead of relying on the external environment and feedback.

Goal Statement

"I will use mind control techniques to boost my self-esteem and solve my problems effectively."

Key Takeaways

1. **You are much stronger than you think you are.**

   You need to focus on the strategies and solutions to help deal with your problems rather than thinking about your problems. If you keep thinking about your problems then you will only waste your time and it's of no use. You should control your mind to solve the problems rather than dwell on them.

2. **You need to get out of your narrow ideas and boost your self-esteem.**

   You need to realize your self-worth and focus on your achievements rather than limiting your ideas and setting boundaries. When you realize your worth, you will be able to experience another kind of freedom and this will increase your self-esteem.

3. **You can improve your self-esteem by focusing on your inner self rather than relying on your external environment.**

   You cannot completely rely on your external factors and environment to increase your self-worth. You should focus on your inner feelings and evaluate yourself to improve your confidence.

4. **If you expect less from yourself than you will get less.**

   You should believe in yourself and have confidence in your abilities. If you doubt your credibility and think that you are not worthy of doing extraordinary things, then you will do the very less of your abilities. You need to focus on your worth and only then you can do your best and can achieve your high goals.

5. **Your boost to your self-esteem is very important for constructive results**

   You need to boost your self-worth by controlling your mind. This will increase your morale and result in positive outcomes. For this, you need to focus on your mind-controlling exercises and know your abilities.

Check for Understanding

Let's check your understanding of the information discussed. Circle the correct answer. Check your answers in the Reference A section.

1. You should limit your thoughts and restrict your abilities to achieve what you want to achieve.

   TRUE   **FALSE**

2. As your life patterns change, your perception of yourselves do not change.

   TRUE   **FALSE**

3. Self-esteem can be improved by focusing on your inner self.

   TRUE   **FALSE**

4. You can boost your self-esteem by concentrating on your inner self rather than your exterior world.

   TRUE   **FALSE**

5. Your achievements in life do not depend on your own perceptions.

   TRUE   **FALSE**

Reflection Questions

1. What behaviors and activities give you a sense of purpose?

   _____

   _____

   _____

   _____

   _____

2. What strategies of yours boost your self-esteem?

_____

_____

_____

_____

_____

_____

_____

3. How can you help people feel confident and capable?

_____

_____

_____

_____

_____

_____

4. Are you satisfied with your current esteem level? Explain your answer.

_____

_____

_____

_____

_____

_____

_____

5. Do you at certain times question yourself? If yes, then elaborate.

_____

_____

_____

_____

_____

_____

_____

Action Plan

With all of this in consideration, make a list of the ways you can challenge yourself and increase your self-esteem. Every day, think about what you want to accomplish. Then, for each day, create reasonable objectives for yourself and keep track of your progress by writing down all of your successes. Reducing your stress by taking time off to do something soothing is a terrific way to start feeling better about yourself. This may be anything from taking a long bath to meditation, gaming, indoor dancing, singing, whatever works for you!

_____

_____

_____

_____

_____

_____

_____

_____

_____

_____

_____

_____

_____

_____

Self-Evaluation

Did doing the action plan boost your self-esteem? What did you decide to do and overall what it a positive experience? Evaluate yourself and congratulate yourself on the milestone you have accomplished so far.

_____

_____

_____

_____

_____

_____

_____

_____

_____

_____

Chapter 19:
MIND CONTROL IN
THE BUSINESS WORLD

Chapter Overview

Mind Control graduates claim they feel fortunate because of their work. Hoffmann-La Roche, Inc., is one of the world's biggest pharmaceutical producers. Graduate: Mind Control offered me a new feeling of understanding about myself and working with others. Some attended courses with employer sponsorship, many on their own. The course leads to enhanced confidence and an overall sense of well-being, say, participants. Chicago-based Idea Banque, Inc. is a cooperative for Mind Control graduates with patentable innovations.

Goal Statement

"I will try to do my utmost best to improve my memory and cognitive functions."

Key Takeaways

1. **If anything can go wrong, it will, and at the worst possible moment," only to learn that there is really no such rule but rather the cosmic Bill of Rights that Jose spoke about.**

   Graduates of the Mind Control program claim that when their theories are put into practice, this is what occurs. The jobless find employment; the salesperson discovers consumers who are more receptive to him, and the scientist discovers brisk solutions to vexing issues.

2. **Michael Higgins, Director of Employment Development at the Hoffmann-La Roche, Inc., facility in Nutley, New Jersey, asserts that employers are pleased with the graduates of Mind Control because of their upbeat attitudes and cheerfulness.**

   Graduates of Hoffmann-La Roche, Inc.'s Mind Control program in Nutley, New Jersey are taught how to employ mind control to enhance their mental health. According to the head of job development at the organization, the students' upbeat demeanor and attitude benefit their employers.

3. **"I found the participants in the research course to be especially fascinating. They were first the most fervent scorners, but they later proved to be the most passionate of all, "Higgins said**

   "I found the participants in the research course to be especially fascinating. They were first the most vocal skeptics, but they later became the most enthusiastic of all "said Mr. Higgins. Following are some remarks made by Hoffmann-La Roche Mind Control grads that were included in the facility's publication, Inside Roche: Merchandising director's statement: "It helped me have a fresh perspective on who I am and the value of collaborating and communicating with co-workers. I am supplying what I learned by attempting to improve the ability to channel my interests and achievements so there is less wasted time and motion."

4. **The Idea Banque, Inc., a co-op for Mind Control graduates with patentable innovations, is a company developed entirely from the bottom up using Mind Control tactics.**

A co-op in Chicago called The Idea Banque, Inc. is for Mind Control graduates with patentable innovations. It all began when Richard Herro sought to test if the type of intuition that Alpha and Theta triggered might provide useful solutions. With 10 years of expertise as a marketing consultant behind him, Mr. Herro already had a decent response—it had just taken him ten years to figure it out.

5. **Once a month, the group gathers to discuss problems through meditation. Members are people who have business-oriented ideas.**

Every month, the team gets together to use meditation to solve problems. Members are people who have business-oriented ideas. They provide an upfront charge, a modest monthly fee, and a cut of the revenue. An investing club is or was another company started by Mind Control alumni in the Chicago region. A stockbroker believed that using his new capacity to travel across time may help him choose stocks. If through meditation you foresee a stock, purchase it now and sell it afterward. Mr. Herro found the strategy appealing; thus, a club was established. The broker, Mr. Herro, and the other participants were hopeful yet unsure.

Check for Understanding

Let's check your understanding of the information discussed. Circle the correct answer. Check your answers in the Reference A section.

1. According to the organization's head of career development, the student's positive attitude and manner assist their employers.
    TRUE   **FALSE**

2. The Idea Banque, Inc. is a co-op in Chicago for Mind Control graduates with patented technologies.
    TRUE   **FALSE**

3. Every month, the team does not meet to tackle difficulties via meditation. Members are individuals with entrepreneurial ideas.
    TRUE   **FALSE**

4. The mental screen is an amazing method for simultaneously strengthening memory and imagery.
    TRUE   **FALSE**

5. If you use your mental screen to imagine a previous event that occurred surrounding the occurrence you believe you've forgotten, the incident will be there.
    TRUE   **FALSE**

Reflection Questions

1. How do you think anyone should maintain the decorum of a workplace?

_____

_____

2. How important is it for you to have boundaries in the professional world?

_____

_____

_____

_____

_____

_____

_____

3. Have you ever come across a manipulative employer? If yes, then elaborate.

_____

_____

_____

_____

_____

_____

4. Are You Being Influenced or manipulated?

_____

_____

_____

_____

_____

_____

_____

5. Share some of your memory of the time when somebody you knew used mind control.

_____

_____

_____

_____

_____

_____

_____

Action Plan

Now that you know how people use the mind control technique in the business world. Concentrate your attention and avoid trying these manipulations. If needed try the meditative techniques.

Self-Evaluation

Evaluate yourself and see how this habit of mindfulness has saved you from these manipulative mind control techniques that the business world uses. Do a self-evaluation and see whether this information has helped you.

_____

_____

_____

_____

_____

_____

_____

_____

_____

_____

_____

_____

_____

_____

_____

_____

_____

_____

_____

_____

_____

Chapter 20:
WHERE DO WE GO FROM HERE?

Chapter Overview

The chapter aims to summarize the mind control techniques and encourage you to explore new ideas. You can achieve what you can imagine by knowing your self-worth and having confidence in your abilities. You need to start focusing on yourself, and you can do better. Your mind has the capacity to do miracles and you just have to start practicing these mind control techniques in order to make it your habit.

Goal Statement

"I will practice mind control techniques and explore new potentials."

Key Takeaways

1. **You can explore new achievements by using mind control techniques**

   There is no limit to knowledge and you always find new developments within your previous knowledge. You can practice using mind control techniques and one day you will become a master of some techniques which you will use in your daily life.

2. **In order to get out of your mind control, you need to view your problems as projects and try to solve them according to your wish.**

   You can succeed in controlling your mind by taking your problems as tasks and solving them as you want them to be solved. By doing this you will relieve yourself from the stress and anxiety. Also, you will experience a sense of control over your mind which will enable you to perform better.

3. **With proper training you will be able control your mind without making a conscious effort.**

   You have to practice mind control techniques so that you can make it part of your daily routine. In this way, you can make mental screens immediately and will be able to take shortcuts to solve any matter of concern by controlling your mind effectively.

4. **You are your own researcher.**

   You have unlimited capabilities to explore new things and techniques. You need to focus on yourself. You can achieve much more than what you have achieved so far. You have 24 hours a day and you have a mind which can accomplish much more than you can ever imagine. Start exploring yourself and your abilities and you will be astonished at the results.

5. **You have to start concentrating on your abilities and focus on what you can do more.**

   You have so much potential to achieve in your life. You just need to believe in yourself and you can do wonders. You need to focus on your abilities and your worth in order to fully utilize your strength.

Check for Understanding

Let's check your understanding of the information discussed. Circle the correct answer. Check your answers in the Reference A section.

1. New potentials cannot be achieved if you start focusing on your mind control techniques.

   TRUE   **FALSE**

2. Your mind can achieve much more than you can even imagine.

   TRUE   **FALSE**

3. If you start practicing mind control techniques you can make it part of your daily routine.

   TRUE   **FALSE**

4. You can practice mind control technique only if you are willing to help others.

   TRUE   **FALSE**

5. You have to concentrate on your abilities and potentials to achieve your high goals.

   TRUE   **FALSE**

Reflection Questions

1. Have you practiced any mind controlling technique?

   _____

   _____

   _____

   _____

   _____

2. How are you planning to start concentrating on your self-worth?

_____

_____

_____

_____

_____

_____

_____

3. What is your opinion on the idea of taking your problems as projects?

_____

_____

_____

_____

_____

_____

_____

4. Have you done any kind of mental exercise to relax your mind?

_____

_____

_____

_____

_____

_____

_____

5.   How can you explore your potential and strengths?

_____

_____

_____

_____

_____

_____

_____

Action Plan

Consideration all the mind-controlling techniques you need to ponder about yourself, write down your strengths and abilities. You were asked to do this earlier in the workbook, but perhaps now you have a different perspective. Believe in yourself and concentrate on your self-worth. Set new goals for yourself and try to achieve them. You are doing great and you can do a lot better.

_____

_____

_____

_____

_____

_____

Self-Evaluation

What will be your plan for boosting your confidence and self-worth? How do you think these mind controlling techniques will help you in your daily life? What will be your way forward after reading all the mind controlling techniques?

_____

_____

_____

_____

_____

_____

_____

_____

_____

_____

_____

_____

_____

_____

_____

_____

_____

_____

_____

_____

Background Information About Jose Silva

José Silva (August 11, 1914 – February 7, 1999) was born in Texas and ran a thriving electronics-repair business for forty years. He was an American self-taught parapsychologist and the creator of the "Silva Method" and the "Silva Ultra Mind ESP System," which aimed to help people increase their IQ, develop psychic abilities, and develop the ability to heal themselves and others remotely using forces unknown to science. In the 1940s, he began experimenting with psychic powers and brain wave activity, eventually inventing The Silva Mind Control Method and a variety of teaching courses and programs. The Silva Method is still taught at seminars and events by licensed instructors, as well as through home-study courses. He passed away in 1999.

Silva created a series of tactics in the 1940s with the goal of altering his children's IQs and developing their psychic talents. His mind experiments were based on his background in electronics and psychology reading. He'd researched alpha waves and electrical activity in the human brain and purchased an electroencephalograph (EEG). He discovered that one portion of the brain, the one that generates alpha brain wave activity, was more powerful than the others. This told him that the electrical impedance of this part of the brain was lower, and so it would work more efficiently.

Reference A

Check for Understanding Answer Key

CHAPTER 1

    1. **TRUE**   2. **FALSE**   3. **TRUE**   4. **TRUE**   5. **FALSE**

CHAPTER 2

    1. **FALSE**   2. **FALSE**   3. **TRUE**   4. **FALSE**   5. **FALSE**

CHAPTER 3

    1. **TRUE**   2. **FALSE**   3. **FALSE**   4. **FALSE**   5. **TRUE**

CHAPTER 4

    1. **FALSE**   2. **TRUE**   3. **TRUE**   4. **TRUE**   5. **TRUE**

CHAPTER 5

    1. **TRUE**   2. **FALSE**   3. **FALSE**   4. **FALSE**   5. **TRUE**

CHAPTER 6

    1. **FALSE**   2. **TRUE**   3. **TRUE**   4. **FALSE**   5. **TRUE**

CHAPTER 7

    1. **TRUE**   2. **TRUE**   3. **FALSE**   4. **TRUE**   5. **TRUE**

CHAPTER 8

    1. **FALSE**   2. **FALSE**   3. **TRUE**   4. **TRUE**   5. **FALSE**

CHAPTER 9

   1. **TRUE**   2. **TRUE**   3. **FALSE**   4. **FALSE**   5. **TRUE**

CHAPTER 10

   1. **FALSE**   2. **TRUE**   3. **TRUE**   4. **FALSE**   5. **TRUE**

CHAPTER 11

   1. **TRUE**   2. **FALSE**   3. **TRUE**   4. **TRUE**   5. **FALSE**

CHAPTER 12

   1. **FALSE**   2. **FALSE**   3. **TRUE**   4. **FALSE**   5. **FALSE**

CHAPTER 13

   1. **TRUE**   2. **FALSE**   3. **FALSE**   4. **FALSE**   5. **TRUE**

CHAPTER 14

   1. **FALSE**   2. **TRUE**   3. **TRUE**   4. **TRUE**   5. **TRUE**

CHAPTER 15

   1. **TRUE**   2. **FALSE**   3. **FALSE**   4. **FALSE**   5. **TRUE**

CHAPTER 16

No True False Questions

CHAPTER 17

   1. **TRUE**   2. **TRUE**   3. **FALSE**   4. **TRUE**   5. **TRUE**

CHAPTER 18

   1. **FALSE**   2. **FALSE**   3. **TRUE**   4. **TRUE**   5. **FALSE**

CHAPTER 19

1. **TRUE**   2. **TRUE**   3. **FALSE**   4. **FALSE**   5. **TRUE**

CHAPTER 20

1. **FALSE**   2. **TRUE**   3. **TRUE**   4. **FALSE**   5. **TRUE**

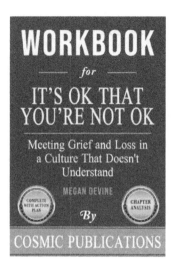

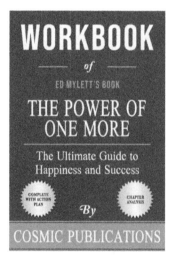

THANK YOU FOR FINISHING THE BOOK!

Looks like you've enjoyed it! :)

We here at Cosmic Publications will always strive to deliver to you the highest quality guides. So, we would like to thank you for supporting us and reading until the very end.

Before you go, would you mind leaving us a review on Amazon? It will mean a lot to us and support us creating high quality guides for you in the future.

Thank you again.

Warmly,

The Cosmic Publications Team

Made in United States
Orlando, FL
28 November 2022